What on Earth
Life in the
Desert

What on Earth?

What a scorcher!

The hottest desert in the world is the Sahara in Africa. At the hottest point in the day the sand is so hot it can burn through the skin on the soles of your feet in seconds.

So how does anything survive in a desert?

Find out in this book.

First published in 2005 by
Book House an imprint of
The Salariya Book Company
25 Marlborough Place
Brighton
BN1 1UB

HB ISBN 1-905087-37-3
PB ISBN 1-905087-38-1

Visit our website at **www.book-house.co.uk**
for free electronic versions of:
You Wouldn't Want to be an Egyptian Mummy!
You Wouldn't Want to be a Roman Gladiator!
Avoid joining Shackleton's Polar Expedition!
Avoid Sailing on a 19th-Century Whaling Ship!

Due to the changing nature of internet links, The Salariya Book Company
has developed an online list of websites related to the subject of this book.
This site is updated regularly. Please use this link to access the list:
http://www.book-house.co.uk/WOE/desert

A catalogue record for this book is available from the British Library.

Printed and bound in China.

Editor:	Ronald Coleman
Senior Art Editor:	Carolyn Franklin
DTP Designer:	Mark Williams

Picture Credits Julian Baker: 2, 3, 6, 7, 8(t), 9, 16, 19(t),
24(t), Elizabeth Branch: 8(b), 9(b), Mark Bergin: 19(b),
24(b), A.N.T Photo Library: 20(b), Mike Lane, NHPA: 21,
Free Agents LTD, Corbis: 25(b), Digital Vision: 10, 11, 12,
13, 14, 15, 17, 22, 23, 25(t), 27, 31, PhotoDisc: 18, 28,
PhotoSpin.com: 20(t), John Foxx: 26, 29

What on Earth?

Tricky toads

When caught in a predator's
mouth, a horny toad squirts
blood. This tastes so bad
that the toad is dropped,
giving it a chance of escape.

What on Earth?

Life in the Desert

GERALD LEGG

How does this land turn into this desert?

Turn to page 16 and find out!

BOOK HOUSE

Contents

What on Earth?

32

Desert tricks?

In a hot desert, desperate travellers can be fooled into thinking they see an oasis. As they rush towards it, it vanishes. This is called a 'mirage', - it is a trick of the light.

Introduction

A desert is defined as land with less than 25 cm (10 in) of rain a year. Many hot deserts have no rain at all for years. Some deserts only have fogs and heavy dews. Desert days are very hot but the nights are **very** cold! It is not just heat that dries the desert but it is also the wind. Strong winds from the Sahara Desert in North Africa can blow sand as far away as southern Italy - about 1,000 kilometres (621 miles).

Is there ever water in a desert?

Most desert rain falls during very violent thunderstorms. River-beds that have been dry and cracked for months or even years can quickly fill to become fast-flowing rivers.

What happens when the storm is over?

Seeds and plant roots that have been waiting for rain now **burst** into life filling the desert with flowers and insects. They must complete their life cycles quickly before the desert becomes too hot and dry again.

What is a desert?

Imagine a desert. What do you see - nothing but sand with a baking hot sun overhead? No - not all deserts are hot. Some are always cold like the desert on Antarctica around the South Pole. There the sun is never overhead, and the desert is too cold for anything to grow. So how can deserts be in very hot regions and very cold regions? Deserts, whether hot or cold, are always very dry places.

Animals in hot deserts usually rest until night when it is cooler. To cope with the heat and lack of water, most desert animals do not sweat. Creatures like the kangaroo rat never drink. They get all their liquid from their food.

Gila woodpecker

Coyote

Desert scorpion

Kit fox

Rattlesnake

Kangaroo rat

6

American kestrel

Saguaro cactus

Costa's hummingbird

Elf owl

Burrowing owl

Desert spiny lizard

Monarch butterfly

Mule deer

Jack rabbit

Spiny lizard

Gila monster

Where are deserts?

There are deserts on each of Earth's continents, although Europe's desert in central Spain is rather small to be called a 'proper' desert. The Sahara Desert in Africa is the largest on Earth and covers almost as much land as the whole USA.

North America

Atlantic Ocean

Pacific Ocean

South America

Antarctica

■ **Areas of desert shown on these maps.**

Which North American desert is the largest?

North America has five main deserts. The best-known is the Painted Desert with the spectacular Grand Canyon running through it. The other deserts are the Great Basin, the Sonoran, the Mojave and the Chihuahua Desert of Mexico, which is the largest of the five.

Jack rabbit   Chuckwalla   Sage grouse

Is Australia the driest continent?

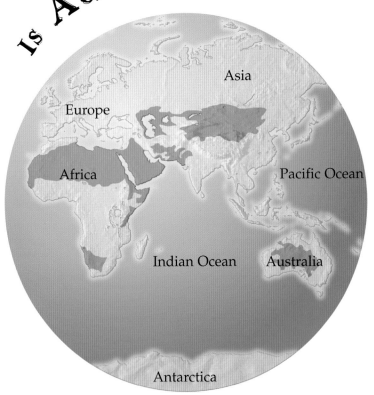

No. Antarctica is even drier than Australia, but because they are both so dry, they have large deserts. But Antarctica's desert is very cold and Australia's is very hot. Many Europeans died exploring Australia's 'outback' (its deserts).

Which desert is more rock than sand?

The Sahara Desert. Surprisingly it actually has more rock and gravel than sand!

Which desert is the size of France?

Rub' al Khali is the largest desert in Saudi Arabia. It is known as the Empty Quarter because nothing lives there. It is about the size of France!

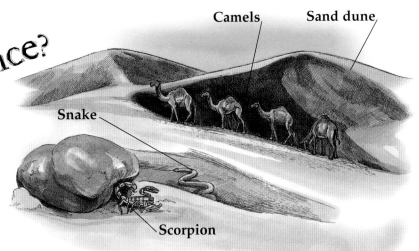

Are all deserts sandy?

Most deserts have sand but deserts also have large areas covered in gravel or rocks. Plants could not grow in deserts without stony areas. Why? Sand is always shifting in the desert winds, so plants have no time to put down roots and grow. Plants need water too which would soak straight through sand.

Where does the rain go?

When rain soaks through the sand it reaches hard rock and it becomes an underground stream. These streams can bubble up in stony areas of the desert. Here brilliant green, leafy plants grow. The plants and water attract animals, insects, birds - and humans. This fertile area in a desert is called an oasis. If an oasis dries up, the plants and trees die and people move on. Soon only the skeletons of trees remain.

What on Earth? Rain, what's that?

In 1971, rain fell in the Atacama Desert in northern Chile for the first time in **400 years!** The Atacama is the world's driest desert.

Why are deserts dry?

Deserts are dry because very little moisture reaches them. Wind blowing over warm seas picks up moisture which falls as rain when it reaches land. By the time wind reaches the centre of a continent it has no moisture left and is dry. It is dry winds like this that have created the Gobi Desert in central Asia and Australia's Simpson Desert.

Which desert is the size of Disney World?

The Navajo Nation's Monument Valley Park in Nevada, USA covers an area as big as Disney World, Florida.

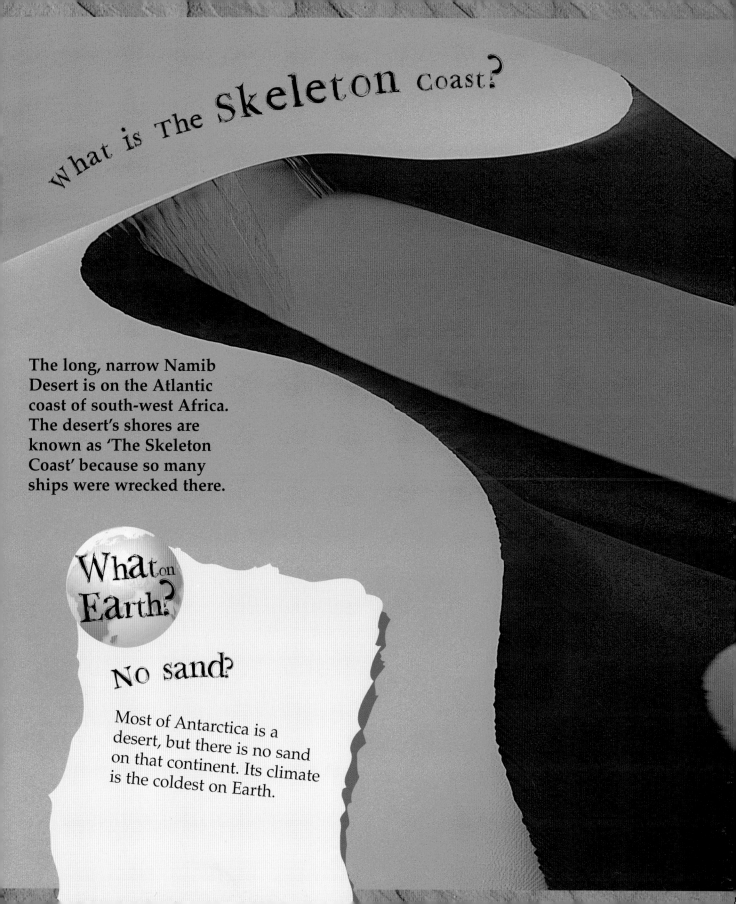

What is The Skeleton Coast?

The long, narrow Namib Desert is on the Atlantic coast of south-west Africa. The desert's shores are known as 'The Skeleton Coast' because so many ships were wrecked there.

What on Earth?

No sand?

Most of Antarctica is a desert, but there is no sand on that continent. Its climate is the coldest on Earth.

Have there always been deserts?

There have always been deserts on Earth but not always where they are now. Over millions of years the Earth's climate has gone through cycles of warm and cold periods which have changed its landscape. Archaeologists have found the bones of woolly **mammoths** in southern England, yet they would only have lived in very cold places. So England must once have been much, much colder.

What is The Mexican Hat?

The cliffs of Zion in the Great Basin Desert are over 136 million years old. Over time, the rocks have been eroded to form strange shapes like 'The Mexican Hat' (below).

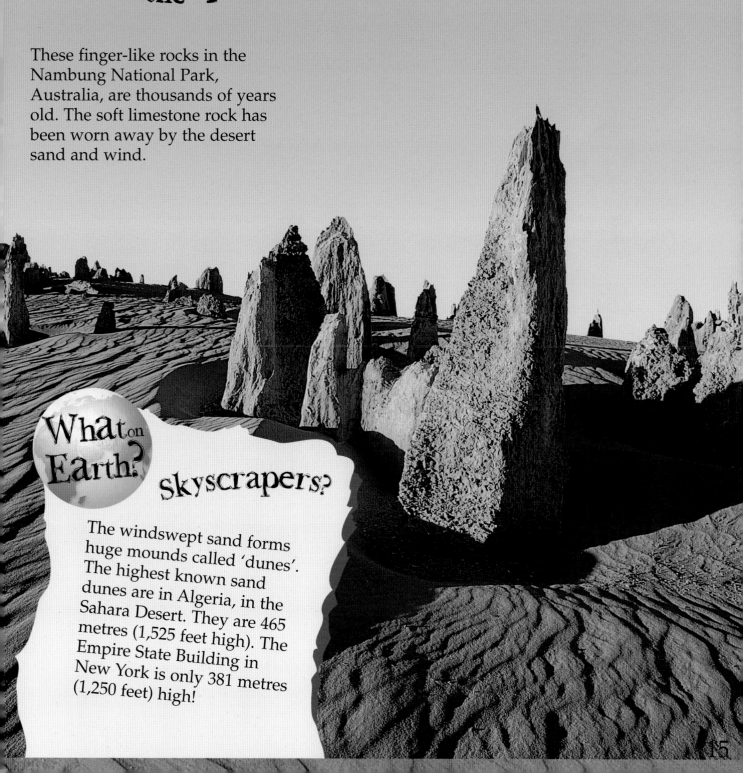

why do the rocks look like this?

These finger-like rocks in the Nambung National Park, Australia, are thousands of years old. The soft limestone rock has been worn away by the desert sand and wind.

What on Earth? Skyscrapers?

The windswept sand forms huge mounds called 'dunes'. The highest known sand dunes are in Algeria, in the Sahara Desert. They are 465 metres (1,525 feet high). The Empire State Building in New York is only 381 metres (1,250 feet) high!

Do deserts grow or shrink?

Over time deserts can grow or shrink. At present more deserts are growing than shrinking. A desert will spread when vegetation at its edges is killed off by drought. Without vegetation to protect it, the soil is blown or washed away and the land becomes a desert.

How does land become a desert?

1

Where there is rain and the soil is rich, plants and animals can live and grow. People settle in such places to work and farm.

2

If forests are cut down and cleared for crops, grazing and firewood, the soil is left exposed to the sun and wind.

3

The soil disappears, blown away by the wind or washed away in flash floods. If the land is overgrazed, only poor, scrubby plants can survive - the land becomes arid.

4

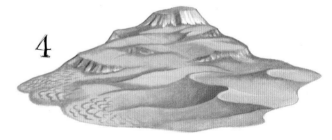

Fires and strong winds cause damage that help deserts to spread. If the rains fail and wells and springs run dry, the land becomes barren.

Is the Sahara desert moving?

What on Earth?

Buried city?

The Sahara's sand dunes are spreading towards Nouakchott, the capital city of Mauritania in Africa, and threaten to engulf it.

The area known as the Sahara Desert was not always a desert. During the Roman Empire, from about 27 BC to AD 350 the Sahara was a rich farming region and supplied the Roman Empire with most of its grain. In the last 50 years the Sahara Desert has grown by about 4 kilometres (2.5 miles) a year.

Riches in the desert?

Deserts are harsh places to live, but treasure may lie under them. The main treasure is oil. Like coal, oil forms over **millions** of years from the remains of plants and animals. This shows that areas we now know as deserts were once covered in thick forests, lush vegetation and shallow seas.

What on Earth?

Armoured lizard?

The armadillo lizard's armoured body gives it complete protection. When in danger it rolls itself up with its tail held tightly in its jaws to protect its soft belly.

Garnet Gold Sapphire

Silver

Salt

Topaz

Uncut
diamond Amethyst Emerald

The desert is also rich in precious metals and gems, including copper, gold, silver, uranium and diamonds. Natural salts called gypsum and borates are processed and used in building materials, glass and pottery. Drug companies also make use of them.

What on Earth?

Old jewels!

Precious stones called opals are mainly mined in Australia. Opals were formed 15 to 30 million years ago.

Armoured tanks are used during desert wars. Thick metal plates help to protect the soldiers inside.

Armoured tank!

How do desert animals survive?

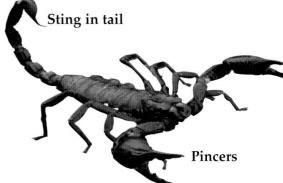
Sting in tail

Pincers

A desert animal's life is very hard. The heat and lack of water are its biggest problems. Most creatures shelter from the heat of the sun and appear only at night. Many burrow underground. They have had to adapt to survive in the desert.

Scorpions detect the tiniest movements of their prey. They grab it with large pincer-like claws and inject a deadly venom from the sting in their tail.

Which lizard inflates?

The thorny devil from Australia inflates when attacked. It drinks dew that collects on its skin. Other lizards lick dew from plants and stones.

Thorny devil

What on Earth?

Why rattle?

The Eastern diamond-back is the largest rattlesnake at two metres (6.5 feet) long. It shakes the tip of its tail (its rattle) to scare off enemies.

Many snakes hunt at night. They sense the body heat of their prey even in total darkness.

Ship of the desert?

Camels are called 'ships of the desert' because they are so well adapted to life there. They can travel for long distances without food or water. Like many desert animals they don't lose water needlessly by sweating. The dromedary camel has one hump and the bactrian camel has two humps.

Nostrils can be closed almost completely in a sandstorm

Long eyelashes to protect its eyes from sand and sun

The hump is full of fat, a built-in supply of fluid to nourish the camel over long distances

Ears can flatten for protection in a sandstorm

Thick knee pads for kneeling and resting

Tough lips that can grip thorny plants

A camel's huge stomach holds an enormous amount of food and water. It can drink 114 litres (200 pints) of water at one go. An average car holds 60 litres of petrol.

Long sturdy legs make camels good runners

Wide, padded feet which splay out help to stop the camel sinking into the sand

How do plants survive in the desert?

Plants have adapted to survive the deserts' harsh conditions. Hairs and prickly spines protect plants like cacti from heat and stops animals eating them. Plants have long roots to search out water and tough skins to stop moisture escaping.

Giant saguaro cactus

What on Earth?

Cactus fountain?

Cacti are only found in the deserts of North and South America. When a giant saguaro cactus is 10 metres (33 feet) tall, it can contain huge amounts of liquid.

How long did this arm take to grow?

The giant saguaro cactus, found only in the Sonoran Desert in the USA, can live for up to 200 years. It takes between 75-100 years for one cactus arm to grow.

fridge or tree?

When a kokerboom tree dies its trunk is hollowed out and used to keep food fresh because it acts as a natural fridge. The Khoikhoi bushmen of Namibia in Africa make arrow quivers from its branches.

How do people live in deserts?

Deserts may be harsh, but people have lived in them for at least 300,000 years. Nomads are desert people who live in temporary tent like structures. They move from place to place in search of food and water. Their clothes help them to stay cool and protect them from the wind-blown sand.

Mongolians in central Asia and Bedouins in Arabia are both nomadic tribes.

Mongolian Yurt

Yurts look more like portable huts than tents. Thick layers of felt are laid over a wooden frame.

Do Bedouins travel light?

The nomadic Bedouins of the Sahara Desert travel long distances with everything they own strapped on the backs of camels.

Bedouin tent Bedouins live in tents made of goats' hair cloth. They are light and easy to put up.

Chilly nights brrr!

The Gobi Desert in Asia is bitterly cold at night. The temperature can fall to -40° centigrade (-40° fahrenheit).

Off-road vehicles driving in the desert destroy the sand dunes and fragile desert soils.

When did Aborigines reach Australia?

Aborigines reached the continent of Australia 50,000 to 60,000 years ago. Since then they have learned to live in harmony with its harsh climate. Their life is closely linked to the land, its animals, plants and the world of spirits. To the Aborigines, everything in the world is important and is worthy of respect.

Hot and cold, what are the dangers in the desert?

Deserts are dangerous places and water is the key to survival. Your body can lose 3 litres (5 pints) of water in just one hour. Your body also loses salt as you sweat and this weakens you and can cause painful cramps and even death.

What on Earth? Dust devils?

Dust devils look like small tornadoes. They suck up sand and dust as they spin across the desert. These sand-filled columns of hot air can be 805 metres (half a mile) high.

How would you survive in the desert?

Look for any shade by day and travel at night when it is cooler. Use the stars to help you to navigate. Water is much more important than food in the desert. So take things slowly and do not waste your energy.

Desert Dangers

Panicking If you are lost in the desert, panicking will only make the problem worse. Think calmly, consider your options and decide on a plan.

Sun stroke Early symptoms are panting and drooling. Loosen clothing, find shelter and submerge yourself in cool water...if you can find any!

Rattlesnakes Although rattlesnakes try to avoid human contact, they kill over a dozen people in the USA every year. If bitten keep warm and call emergency services immediately.

What to take Check-list

A **Hat** keeps the sun off your head and protects your neck from sunburn. **Sunglasses** with special dark lenses will protect eyes from the harsh glare of the sun. **Strong boots and thick socks** stop your feet being rubbed by the sand. A **Scarf** to protect your face in case of a sand-storm. Remember **Sun cream** to protect your skin in the day and a **Warm jacket** for those cold nights.

Desert facts

Desert sand grains are round, unlike water-worn sand grains found on beaches.

Avalanches don't only occur in snowy regions. If a sand dune collapses it is called an avalanche.

A sand dune avalanche can be heard as far as 10 kilometres (6 miles) away.

Walking across sand is not easy many desert rodents jump instead.

Cactus

The Qaidam Depression, in China is the highest desert in the world. It is 2,600 metres (1.5 miles) above sea level.

The world's highest temperature, 58°C (136°F), was recorded in the Sahara Desert.

The Sahel region in Africa became a desert in the 1970s due to drought and over farming.

A bactrian camel has a thick fur coat for warmth in the cold Gobi Desert. In Summer it sheds its fur and becomes almost hairless.

The Rub' al-Khali Desert in southern Arabia is the longest area of continuous sand in the world.

The sand lizard (Namib Desert) lifts its legs up and down from the burning sand or lies on its stomach to raise all four legs at once.

Glossary

Archaeologist A person who studies earlier times from the remains that are left.

Antarctic A continent covered in ice at the bottom of the globe.

Arid Land that is too dry for plants to grow.

Barren Land that can no longer support life.

Continent One of the Earth's main land masses.

Dromedary Camel with one hump.

Erosion Gradual wearing away of something.

Flash flood Sudden flood that can occur in deserts. If the ground has been baked so hard that the rain cannot soak through, the water pours over the surface.

Moisture Damp air.

Nomad Someone who moves from place to place, usually in search of food for their animals.

Oil Thick, sticky liquid obtained from the ground.

Overgrazing Keeping too many grazing animals, like cows, sheep and goats, on the same land for too long damages the plants and may lead to erosion of the ground.

Male hooded oriole

29

What do you know about the desert?

1   What is the largest desert in the world?

2   What is the driest desert in the world?

3   When is an area called a desert?

4   What valuable black liquid is found under some deserts?

5   What should you do to survive in a desert?

6   Why does a cactus have prickly spines?

7   What is the largest desert in North America?

8   Why does a rattlesnake 'rattle'?

9   What is in a camel's hump?

10 What is a mirage?

Go to page for 32 for the answers!

What is this rock called?

Go to page for 32 for the answer!

Index

Pictures are shown in **bold** type

Answers

1. The Sahara in North Africa. (See page 8)
2. The Atacama Desert, in Chile (See page 11)
3. When a place has less than 25 cm (10 in) of rain each year. (See page 5)
4. Oil. (See page 15)
5. Stay calm and cover your skin and head. (See page 27)
6. To protect against heat and to stop animals eating them. (See page 22)
7. The Chihuahuan Desert in Mexico. (See page 8)
8. To frighten enemies away. (See page 20)
9. A store of fat. (See page 21)
10. An illusion that makes distant objects appear much closer. (See page 4)

The Devil's Marbles are a collection of gigantic rounded granite boulders, many of which are precariously balanced on top of one another. Scattered heaps of these marbles occur across a wide, shallow valley north of Alice Springs, Australia.